Twenty Colors

Twenty Colors

poems by
Elizabeth Kirschner

Carnegie Mellon University Press
Pittsburgh 1992

Acknowledgments

Crab Creek Review: "The Night of the Falling Comets"
The Georgia Review: "Built With the Same Beauty"
The Gettysburg Review: "Grandmother's Arms"
Grolier Prize Annual: "My Mother's Door", "The Fifth Season"
The North American Review: "Two Blue Swans"
North Dakota Quarterly: "Twenty Colors", "The Fall of Light",
"A Person Broken in Two", "The Dinosaur's Bone"
The Ohio Review: "Not Far From Here"
Red Cedar Review: "Red Leaves"
Three Rivers Poetry Journal: "Their Asking", "The Life of a
Hummingbird", "The Essential Universe", "The Blueness of
Stars", "This Dusk"

Grateful acknowledgment is made to the Massachusetts Artists
Fellowship program for a Finalist Award which helped to
support the writing of this book.

The author also wishes to thank Robert Wolff and Megan
Elberty for their love and support.

Publication of this book is supported by grants from the National En-
dowment for the Arts in Washington, D.C., a Federal agency, and from
the Pennsylvania Council on the Arts.

Carnegie Mellon University Press books are distributed by Cornell
University Press Services.

Library of Congress Catalog Card Number 91-72057
ISBN 0-88748-128-0
ISBN 0-88748-129-9(Pbk.)

Contents

I.

This Dusk

Brightens the buildings
one block over.
The leaves on the sycamore
turn like mirrors
and cast back the light
I gave away today.

This is a shared universe:
air broken like bread,
words sent from one mouth to another.
Listen
the little voices of us all
are becoming something great
something better
than the separate life each body holds
than the batch of birds
just now
rising.

Not Far From Here

Before me is a tree
with joints smooth as those
of the body, so much so
I want to reach up and place
my hand there, knowing
sex could rouse the limbs like dark
flames thrown freely. I touch
one body after another,
in dreams, in life:
man, tree, heightened sky.

Along the street we're intimate as wounds:
a little Oriental girl in white
underwear and red shoes
twirls a frilly umbrella while standing
near the curb,
a middle-aged man bends over to pick up
the evening paper on his porch. Beyond him,
is a building choked with ivy:
hidden in the mess of green
birds chirp—
rich-voiced, complex in manner as light
or love.

Warm, autumnal evenings are a mistaken
tenderness. One that I fall for
headlong into the belief, sweet
as this lingering light, that we are not
strangers. Yet, not far from here
and not long ago, an old woman, 76,

was beaten to death in her building:
on the landing of the 4th floor.
They followed a trail of blood
to find her. We are all
on the scent now.

Whoever I once was, like that woman
she is long gone from the heart of me.
As I walk up the stairs to my apartment,
I remember my father, who only yesterday
stopped at each landing, blue as a ghost,
to catch his breath. Without thinking,
my hand flutters under my black shirt
to my breast. It's warm.
The nipple is a dark star
couched in unimaginable softness. I climb
higher: beyond the bare tree
of my father's body, beyond
the memory of this dying light
and all the wounds of earth
to where the girl, strange as day,
twirls her umbrella
in utter delight.

The Blueness of Stars

The stars, the implacable stars
stay where they are
because it is
so— one design
worn to dust
like the rug in the foyer
of my childhood home.

That foyer was cold as a well.
Around the rug, slate formed
a night sky whose circumference
I danced more like a fairy
than an ordinary child.

Each slab of slate was a turtle's back,
a looking glass or palace marble.
Most definitely, a shifting scene,
the escalator that goes up and up...

I could have risen then, bodiless,
dusty as yeast, for I knew bits
of magic, ballet leaps,
levitations

learned at slumber parties.
Anything would have lifted me,

but each morning my legs pumped
under the chair at the breakfast table
as if I were on a swing.
The cinnamon toast I crunched on
were my own wings dusted with desire.

My mother's hair, even then, the color of ash
painted on my forehead at the beginning of Lent.
I wanted to die for her
whenever I stared at that back
bent at the stove on school day mornings
and probably did
as I suffered my way in adulthood.

I loved any man who resembled her
particular cache of shadow—
those whose words were sick
with self-hate, whose bodies
were boards, whose organs
were swimming in drink.

I loved each one singly,
wholly, under the blueness of stars,
forgetting once again,
I was an ordinary
woman who longed,
rightfully, for ordinary love—

my body the fantasy
I could have risen from.

I am my mother's daughter,
after all. Rigid
in conception, stuck as stars.
And although I still love
to make up for the losses,

I've shed her sickness
through the rigors of grief.
Yet, even in daytime
when the sun burns
the wick of that child stuck down deep,
the blueness of stars can
cast its dreamy haze and I begin
to move about again in slow
deliberate circles, numb
as a thumb, this strange
inward, flighty
thing.

A Person Broken in Two

Years later, he offers me paradise.
Too bad he is an old man.
Too bad he has white birds
inside his head, half-starved
with longing. He offers me paradise
as simply as he opens the palm
of his hand. All around the house,
flamingos flame the grass.
I am as beautiful as I once was,
more the woman of waters, of dream,
than a person broken in two
at least twice. I move into his arms,
soft as spring lambs. He once said,
it takes a lifetime to become human,
which is why we lived apart.
We had less love than loneliness.
We had the death of his first wife.
We had the moon eating us up.
We had his two children
carried like bottles of milk
from his doorstep to mine each night.
We never kissed the pain that bloomed
in our fingers. We never buried
the dead— a dog, a woman,
a ram— the hands and paws
and horns of which still prick us
in sleep. He offers me paradise
and with sadness I accept.

On the Night of the Falling Comets

My childhood surrounded me— a version
of myself for each day of those long years—
hundreds of Elizabeths like flowers in a field.
Their faces were sweet as daisies,
but the sky was black, the weather was not
for them. A friend helped me gather them
before it was too late. She knew
this is how we save ourselves, this
endless gathering until bouquets bleed
from our arms. Bowed over in harvest,
our bodies copied the goddess who bridged the sky.

Our work done, we lay down and watched
comets spin off like soft, red roses. The stars
spiralled, the moon was in magnitude. This
may have been the end of the world, but we
observed a whole nighttime of blossom.

It could be years later when I send her
a picture postcard of a woman dipping her toes
in a ghostly bay— peacock tails of color
glimmer on her bare back. All the dark
flowers have fallen from her: one
is pinned to her hair. She washes wounds
wide as boats— huge, blue and blessed.

The Life of a Hummingbird

I lie alongside a bird; we are both
diminutive in size. Perhaps a hummingbird.
Her long yellow beak is shoved down my throat,
as if inside a purple flower.
She is pumping me with song.

Her wings lift, light as lace, as if to make
the music eager. This is the time
of my life. A tiny bird assists me.
I could swallow her, sweet as jello,
but I don't. Only the good

get birds like this. In between
her wings, I see space. I see
a star, a rose. I see the whole

world open. This bird came out of me
like seed; she goes back in as blood.
We both have ruby throats.
We both have dreams, small
and quick as raindrops. She stings
me with song; pinches me awake.

In our nest that is green and wild.
On this earth that hasn't killed us yet.

Twenty Colors

I once lived inside a flower.
Each petal was dark as my mother's hands.
I was happy about those hands.
In this flower, I lived in my nightgown,
danced on pointe like a sad child
who twirls before her bedroom mirror
every night. While I outgrew
this flower, it grew within me.
It became a gift I gave to men.
They came into me as if
into a dark room. They touched
the dancing child, her bloody feet.
Red petals littered the bed sheets.
There are at least twenty colors
in the wind. There are at least
twenty men who love me, whose hands
are trembling flowers ripped
by wind. I can never have enough
of them. I can never
have enough. O flowers! O wind!

These Heady Flowers

I am living deeply now
like the white spider I spy
among the wild roses. She lifts her legs,
moves her small ghostly body across each flower
like moonlight in a house. She is the snowflake
vanishing. Her fall from the dark sky
matters. It is quick and bright.
Her web is a beautiful hope
easily undone, a fabric transient as tears.
She lays it all upon these heady flowers
which for her are the world: flushed,
falling, gorgeous and doomed.

The Floating World

On this blowy mountaintop, the white-throated sparrow
sings, *Don't leave me by myself.* I have been crying
all day. Under the indigo sky, the world
is floating. For miles we traveled nowhere but up.
Even the trees can do no more: each branch
grows crooked and black, many times broken,
sometimes hardly alive. To be abandoned in this life
is a fear so acute it cripples me with pain.
Nights when I wake you like blowy branches,
when I snap like a finger bone. You brought me here.
To the top of the floating world. To listen
to that sorrowing bird and bear the beauty
of these gaunt trees. One patch of sky is vermilion.
Fervent as passion. The sparrow's song gives
with the dark. *I am the one for you,*
she cries into valleys wide as pools
where lights float like blossoms.

II.

The Fall of Light

I believe if I look over my shoulder,
there will be sunlight. I fall for this illusion
every minute or so. It is tedious
and tricky as love. What is not in us,
we want about us. Children. The fall
of light. Love. Once I was small enough
to fit inside my father's pocket. He fed me
orange seeds. I talked to him as though
he were a doll. "Now it's time for bed."
"Now it's time to rise." Obedient father,
what happened to us? How come I grew
to the size of a woman while my love,
small as a marble, rolled oggle-eyed
into the darkness? When I look over my shoulder,
I see mist. Black branches poke out
like the arms of someone deceased.
Up and around, there are birds. I follow
the birds. Their flight, upsweeping
toward light, toward air.

Elephant and Child

Men cut off the faces of elephants
with chainsaws, just
for the ivory tusks. The faces fall
like huge, black orchids.

*

Elephant faces big as clouds
float in the night sky
above me. I love
the elephants. I love them
like a child. *Dumbo. Jumbo.*
Their huge ears flap like wings.
I am wrapped in one of their big
black trunks. We fly
above the earth. Elephant and Child.
Sacred as a painting. One looks
like a peanut. The other is big as grief.

*

I wanted to go through the world
anonymously, loving the innocence
of spiders, feeling my heart match
the thumping of the moths,
white and black, who beat
against the screens each night.
I wanted to keep my body warm.
I wanted the small way

that is good and gentle. Rain
pearling on plants. The fabric
of all things wild drawn about me
like a dress. I ignored that
which wasn't near— the difficult
wars of men, the massive destruction
of countries remote as maps,
because to look at this was unbearable
as a glance back at childhood.

*

To come into this world then,
to be one of its true and trembling members,
is to watch the elephant's face fall.
It is to love that elephant like a child.
It is to know that face
is a big basket of fruit.
It is to watch all that is heaved
from it with one's heart
entirely open.

*

Only then are our souls magnified.
Only then can childhood be stored away
like a rag doll soaked with silent tears.
I can say that I have done this.
I walked in the shadow of the elephant
until the elephant was dead.
I did not want to do this.
But now joy, small as butterflies,
manages to flourish about me.

Red Leaves

Light falls rapidly as estrangement.
What passes between us passes away.
Yesterday, I saw a leaf fall, red
as a mitten. Sometimes the whole day
comes down like that— quiet and small.
Sometimes I feel left behind.
See how the butterflies lift themselves
away: they do so gently as breath.
Soon we will scarcely remember them.
Soon I will hold nothing but red leaves
in my hands. I will look at them
with joy. Because all we are
rivals this: red leaves tossed up
suddenly, like fire, like breath.

At Gilson Pond

The last days of August show us
the blue dragonflies. Their wings never moan
even when they drop like oars in water
deep enough to drown them. It is enough
for them to rise and draw together like a bow.
It is enough to watch them. Once again
we believe we are the first to have seen
anything. No other man and woman
have loved one day like this: so brief
and blue, so uproarious. When it ends,
we will be nothing, we will walk in shadow.
We depend on this. All of it ending—
the shy light of late summer, dragonflies
bright as pansies, the dazzle that delivers us,
like a wild guess, from one day to the next.

Built with the Same Beauty

For once I let the universe be large.
Trees live long before and after me.
They are bent like fathers. My own
is the damaged one with leaves
purple as fruit. Each day
on this earth humbles me
until I grow courteous toward slight
things: bird shadow, low roads
that lead into dusk.

Because it is the end
of summer and my father's life,
I creep into the comforts
of emptiness: the quiet awe
of each drawn breath.

My body and my father's body
were built with the same
beauty in mind. All in his
is in ruin. His hands are cool
as my garden in evening,
where I drink in dark
bins of air, oddly intimate
with the green bodies of plants.
I planned this beauty, but ours—
father, daughter, humankind—
is made from wonder and pain.

To come close to anyone
is to touch all that's mortal:
the thick waists of trees, the parade
of birds up above. I watch
the sun and moon trade places.
How easily these bodies shift from light
to dark and back again— as do we,
though bound in the beautiful
failings of flesh.

Their Asking

This is part of the pain of opening.
All of my body asks for you.
My labia, in their thick and fruitful
orchard; my breasts. Look at how the moon
swells, how the riverbanks are matted
with hazy green growth. All this
before autumn and before dusk.
I loved loneliness. Such a passion
dark as blood. My bones
were arrows leading to the kind
of sad experience most live
to avoid. So I paint you with sighs
meant for women who have given
their bodies all too often.
I know their thighs
are marbled with unspeakable
sorrow. That loveliness
is born of forgiveness—
I forgive my breasts, my lips
above and below, their asking.

III.

The Essential Universe

My cousin hits her child in the night.
The sound of a rug beaten by a brush.
The dust flies. O woman, why?
In your belly a new one is coming.
She will be sad and wise.
In her ears, the primitive rhythm
goes on. It is one
she better learn to dance to.
Sally, Sally, Sally,
your arms fall like drumsticks
on the child who has proven
to be much. Her curls,
dazzling and devilish, bounce
with each blow. In the morning,
I will play with her
forever. Lifting her up
to give her back to God
who, like so many husbands,
is a broad back vanishing
down the drive.

Grandma's Green Bowl

Aunt Dorothy brings it out like a secret.
A bowl green as a snake, decorated with trees
light as whispers. In this bowl
are all the gardens Grandma ever made.
Flowers that thrived on moonlight
and disaster. What she loved was
beauty that couldn't be eaten—
hence, a thousand delectable roses,
heavy as heads. She is still
dropping blooms, simple as a stitch.
They fall from heaven in the dark.
They hit the bowl like pennies
in a well. This bowl is heaped
with heavy scents. It is heaped
with the bones of her children,
pink as a chicken's from which
flesh, light as feathers, has been
plucked. These feathers fall
on both Aunt Dorothy and me—
we grow white with delirium
and grief. For this
is Grandma's green bowl, deep enough
for trees to take hold, for blooms,
for all we never dreamed of
would be eaten.

Grandmother's Arms

A night broken like a piece
of Grandmother's china. Perhaps a teacup
with a handle like some strange, bent
walking stick. A tool for the blind.
An instrument to pick at the body
of the dead. I lift it like one
of the white arms of my grandmother.
Like moonlight if it could be captured.
I hook it to her husband, to her grave.
This handle shaped like an ear,
like the arms of everyone in my family,
snapped at the joint. Bone-white
and elegant. Rolling away is the cup.
Cock-eyed as the moon. Until
I face the daylight of nothingness,
of doom, of dolls. I wanted
Grandmother's arms, their beauty reaching
into the beyond. I wanted
to be held in the love
I feel for her. Instead
I touch the chilly rim
of one of her china cups. I touch
her death pressed like a finger
to my lips. I touch her silence,
the crack running like a scar.

My Mother's Door

I sleep on the floor by the fire.
My hand is in my hair. It has been there
since childhood, since I
as a small girl planted my body like a bone
before my mother's door at night.

*

We are riding our bikes at dusk.
I am 12; my mother 42.
The summer evening leaves us
without luxury. The wheels are turning.
I turn them with my golden legs.
These Catherine wheels. These Elizabeth wheels.

*

Once I heard a woman cry, *I am
my mother*! The room floated away
like the world.

In the children's section
of the branch library, I am taking down books
as though each were filled with her dark love.
It is perpetual. This literature of loss.

The room comes back: the gold couch
on which we sat, school nights only.
Her head is in my lap. Cold
as the moon and lost. Bones from my body

are missing— adrift in the dark scene
of her. I leaf through her hair.
So black and full of curls. This
is a painting: her head
on my stomach— fetal,
bulging— a world I couldn't open.

*

I wanted my mother. There
in the woods with my hands
full of violets. In school with the nuns
descending. In the sadness I kept secret
like my middle name.

All on earth wore it:
the Mary birds. The Mary night.
The Mary mother.

*

Because she couldn't bear herself,
she bore me. She pulled on me
like a cigarette in the dark.

My papery insides glowed. I gave
and gave, wildly. Like moonlight

so appallingly beautiful. Too much
to take.

*

At the end of all giving, is the end
of her. Once my primary color.
My night color. The color of a period
on the page.

On my mother's birthday, a bee
lands on the pink palm
of my hand. I feel it
in my bones. Fear
sweeps through me until I lift

it to the door and, with a gesture
like a blown kiss, blow this bee
away.

The Blue Aquarium

We are sad together. Down in the meadow,
the hooves of spotted horses sink in dark crowns
of mud. The sky is white, white enough
to be a veil for the dead. Autumn has turned warm,
unexpectedly. We have turned inward,
also unexpectedly. In there are animals
running themselves to death. We cling
to their spotted spines, which move like snakes
in water. In the old house on Sprucewood Drive,
I had an aquarium for which I purchased
angel fish. Silver and black, their veils were soon
made ragged by other fish. Each kiss
rips you. In the blue aquarium of the mind.
There the dead are rising, their milky bodies
are the glamorous angel fish. Dropping their veils
as I do my black slip after a long and intoxicating
evening. Here is an autumn meadow.
Here are the dappled horses, their steps
are falling apples. A tangerine mist
is sweeping down the hills. Let it lift us
like the beautiful swimmers we are toward all
in this orange air.

The Tulip Tree

My life breaks up like water.
In it are incomplete animals—
tiny as toys, they scatter among
the broad, gold leaves newly shed
by the tulip tree. I enter a gold sea.
With me is my own woman, fresh
and dark. My own beauty
personal as a flower shipped in a box.
All the doorways I ever stood in
opened like a lid. My eyes shone
while men, one by one, took
me by the hand. Dear Andrew,
Matthew, John. Dear Harry.
Dear love. Like gentlemen, you rose
onto your elbows. Like animals
you cried deep into my sleep.
All that's erotic is classical.
All that's beautiful is tragic.
I once planted yellow lilies
in a garden in the rain.
That was many lovers ago.
I wore peculiar leather boots.
Only the lilies remain. Yes,
they do remain.

By the Sea

I.

Where do I go from here? Most bodies
rub against other bodies. Note the sea
and the silky black rocks. Or the spectacle
of mussels clinging to barnacles. I rub
white maps of air; my shoulders
are snowy egrets. In flight.
In flight. Some birds die
from pure exhaustion. From wing flaps
turned like pages— anxiously, as though
what's next were the matter.
Words carry me. They hurt.
They heal. Up. Down.
Flap, flap. Or suppose language
as a dark ferry laboring across
the magnificent sea. Birds,
by virtue, stay aloft rather than afloat.
Their little bones appear insufficient
to the task. Yet each wing flap
sounds like *awe, awe*.

II.

Every time I sleep I let go
of language, of my body with its insurmountable
need, of the vast and rolling history
of people and myself, of the least
assuming insect, of pearly rocks.
I let go of my lover, the richness

of his voice and his organs,
of a God falling like a beard
of moonlight across my flesh.
My childhood and three red dogs—
Fred, Wolfgang and Rocky—
disappear, as do the faces
of friendly women— Marguerite,
Mimi, Meg. It all goes
in an instant. I am drawn up
like a spark into the cold
and the black. Once more,
I am a mere soul, a mere breath,
taken. Reduced like fish stock
to a broth white and rich.
To fill someone else's cup.

III.

Don't call the body a machine; it's not.
It's an organism and responds organically
to all forms of life. The black kite
may line her nest with plastic and paper,
with rubbish, she may even make this nest
on an island where soldiers are trained
to kill, the island itself may be seen
as a nest in a poisoned harbor once famous
for its waterfall of flowers, for this
is Hong Kong after all, but the kite herself
is not the nest, the soldiers or the harbor.
She is simply a bird, lyrical and daring
when in flight, confined and domestic
when incubating a few, delicate, hot eggs.

She adapts slowly and as best she can:
she has not deceived the world
with the simple requirements
of her biology; the world, however,
has deceived her.

IV.

Where do I turn, then, in a world turning
with or without me? Into the spiral
of my white bones? Into the coloring face
of my lover? Into work which blows clean
each day like snow on glass? Into
the soul swirling like a fish tail
in the moonlight. As though the slight
helpings of pleasure and enjoyment
might sustain us through feasts of grief.
As though the moment when we relax
by the sea watching froth tossed up
like a glass blower's breath might serve
as some eternal anchor. As though rare
words of love were the air
we tuck away each second, letting it rip
behind our ribs, letting it tear
into our blood, letting us be,
be.

IV.

The Dinosaur's Bone

Snow falls. It covers the garden cheaply.
Poor man's mulch. And the poor woman?
She is shovelling your shadow
for nothing. The woman I could love

is brief. Like passing through a store
bright with beautiful goods. Or mating
furiously and deep. It is that shy
child's face before it is struck by her mother

on the street. I stand at the foot
of my driveway. Centuries of dusk
come down. My shovel is full
of whitish grief. I push it, heavy

of heart, into the cold, into
the antique world. Tomorrow I may be cast
into the body of a beautiful woman.
At dawn, I will find her kneeling

in the snow. Some say we resemble birds
not at all. Then why do they
fly into me like a flock
of flaming leaves? The bird carries

in its body the dinosaur's bone.
In mine is my grandmother's finger.
It touches me until I shed
the blue scales of the clawed

and the dead. In the monstrous snow
are the shadows of indestructible creatures.
Reptilian birds. Winged women. My shovel.
My back. My bones.

Blue Candles

Around the house, animals tread the circles
of sacrifice. Deer blush the brown of our hearts.
They eat crackers tossed like blue manna

by your father. The snow cracks; we are small,
godless by choice. The deer aren't.
Their footsteps, perfect and sharp as holly leaves,

mimic shadows from heaven. Blue wax,
from the candles on the table, falls down like a dress.
We, too, are internally nude and blue. Eternally

burning. Faith is in the face of your father: ash,
snow and ash. He will not always be with us.
Nor the candles. Nor the deer. Sometimes

I sit on a stump in the woods. Often
I sit on you in sex. Deep in my soul
is this blue union. A woman in love

with ashen snow. Deer trampling all.

Two Blue Swans

My mother and father are two wounds, hanging
like ear lobes. Each day I pierce them

with jewels: rubies, pearls, tempered bits
of gold. Or think of them as shriveled ovaries

between which I, a blossom of being,
float. My beauty is their manifest.

I am the chance they never had.
Snow monkeys have been known, when their offspring

are stillborn, to carry the corpse with them
for days, even weeks. They nurture the dead.

I clutch the shrunken heads
of my mother and father. Tear them from me

and I will shriek, madly. In my dreams,
two blue swans unfurl magnificently and mate,

and rise. I roll toward my lover in the bed. And so
the moon and snowy rain press

upon my windows. And so my mother and father
tumble like an afterbirth. I let them out

like fabric, like stitches from my flesh.
And so, I am the afterlife, the glow

they felt when young and in love.
When nearing for that first great kiss.

The World's Music

My body is small as a poem. Once
I believed I could carry myself away,

like an infant wounded in the making.
The sky is cloth: pieces of us are torn,

white and jagged. The luxury of the day
lies in its beginning. At my feet

is all the sparkling snow. I wash
the dark linens of my unhappiness,

stiff as doll clothes. Let them freeze
like photographs of war. What do these

pictures tell me? That more than many
die. And women are carved, by hand,

into pipes of grief. O the world's music
is magic. In it are the screams

of birth. Or the dying and the glitter
of their deaths. So high. So low.

And everywhere, green songs
between.

Burning Bouquets

On the winter solstice, my mother holds
her tiny grandchild. Her arms are a crypt.

She bends her death around this child,
lovingly. We have all floated there,

in quiet and belief. Except my father who kneels
before the fire. Those red flowers are the ones he's carried

and passes: *live as the gorgeous flames*
eating up your arms. In the black space

of my being, a woman as a rose, grows: full
and erotic. All night she rises

to pleasure as though heaven, dark
as a blizzard, were upon her. All experience

of love parallels that of snow: swift,
stinging, a blinding glory

that falls and flies.

This Enterprise

We do not feed the wild birds. In the bitter cold,
a downy woodpecker stitches the trees with hunger.
Her feathers are a palatial robe: black, silver

white and grand. Hers is a story of spectacular
survival. Around the house, animal tracks in snow
look like ribbons of scars. As a woman in love

with all, I want one for my body. My scars
come from God: bracelets which slip on
and make a mysterious music. Throughout the woods,

trees are moaning and breaking. Throughout the world,
people do the same. How it became joyous
is beyond me. This enterprise of God and woman

and man; of plants and animals delicious enough
to eat. My body, too, is a dish: I feed
a multitude. The sun is a knife;

the moon, a fork: pillagers all.

V.

The Fifth Season

This morning I nailed a new calendar
to the wall: January, 1990.
My father would say I've begun
my thirty-fifth year. Where
then, has he been?

In his red hands, I see the shape
of a boat. This is how he carried me,
in a dark vessel. On a sea
of no ending: only waves
tossed like nothing. Only melancholia.
Only the parted lips of my grandmother,
thin and alive. Only passage.

I desire these shapes— my father;
my mother holding him. My lover
who lives long on my body. The fifth
season comes in sleep:

birds glutted with moonlight, beauty
which makes me weep. Quick,
painful, luminous. What have I seen
that matters? The short
appearance of these birds.

Who fill trees as fruit
does the mouth. As your tongue
does my body. As words
are only a small part
of experience, so the seasons
close up, like walls.

We live as though captive. Some say
whenever we are mortal,
we are tragic. Above are the minor
and major stars. Or the shadowy body
of the moon. And clouds
heavy with loss. Part them

as you would the legs
of your beloved. In the curly hills
are richly created animals.
And a feast which remains unnamed.

Feed me the fifth season: light
to tear me to pieces. See
the love of my body
float down. In a world
constant with snow
and rain. With all that pours
from people: blood, breath
and sorrow.

        Some say sin
is to live as though limited.
So we have sinned in all. The fifth
season is soul. Vastly grown
and particle by particle,
earned.

The Fullness of Time

Don't trust what you know: know
what you trust— my brother's face, soft
as a stuffed monkey, the floor of the woods
covered with violets, hopping birds.
More obscene than safe— this is the truth
of childhood. For all that's small
is violated: snow underfoot, spiders
dark as time, the faces of my brothers
and sister.

                Winter ends
and the holds of hope fall from me,
like a sleeping child who loosens the grip
she has on her own hair. There is bliss
in nothingness; the mud's upheaval
is a sullen joy. I pass each morning
in silence as though in reverence
or reverie or sorrow.

      A life can pass like this:
letting it all go. Rather, let it all
come.

*

             One January night,
we walked under the full moon, the brightness
streaming through the woods like a dark surprise.
We stripped, that is, half undressed. Snow stuffed
in our boot tops like ghostly orchids. What
or whom did we love? Moon, self,
dreamy snow. The dropped clothing

            as though we were in a room.

*

Rooms, like time, grow within.
The rooms of certain hours, quiet as lids.
The rooms of certain loves, dropping
like flowers. The rooms of childhood,
sacred, shaken: the way snow
is ripped from the roof on windy nights,
as though in scorn. As though
it were my breath.

*

Know what you trust: little
as sunlight on these grey days.

The eternal as seen
in the fullness of time...

*

In time, there is sadness, sweet
as my brother's face. There is loss
breaking like moonlight over my sister
as she sleeps. There is emptiness.
It sweeps through my oldest brother's
body, pure as a secondhand.

*

I'm still the child I've long outgrown,
the one wanting in her hands, the one
who shares loneliness with three siblings
like a single slice of bread.

The bread that multiplies.
Until its crumbs are snow
over our entire world, small
as it may be— a ranch house,
3/4's of an acre, the dogwood trees
whose blossoms my mother inordinately loves.

Once a year those blossoms turn to her,
like ears to hear her sorrow.
Her deep grief takes birds
from their branches. She whispers
like the spring breeze that can almost reach me,
"God has been good to us."

In time, I am grateful.
But never grateful enough.

Second Childhood

I'm still, full and still. Nothing
moves: no windows waxed by the moon, no doors.
No longing left out like silk. My childhood
is at one with the stones. My body weighted
so it doesn't blow away. All the wind is
paper, reams of it aloft, touched by time.
So beauty goes by and by. So the eternal
stops in; a quiet guest.

                All grief is classic:
it comes from classic wounds. My mother and father
who are driving, in the two-tone Buick,
to see my brother in North Carolina.
It's his 40th birthday; my 40 millionth.
It happens whenever I lie down, here
in the moonlight: I blow out my old self.
A candle soft as gum.

*

I enter second childhood, chatting away
as we drive down snow-gushed roads.
It's simple: the stars are in the emptiness
which makes their light, light. Hence
my voice. Or the stitches I took
in your blue robe, earlier in the day.
While snow fell like sudden light, the stove
groaned and burned, groaned and burned:
the needle moved through the cloth with ease.
Like a boat through the forest green ocean.
Like me through the wholeness of soul.

*

This childhood is erotic. I cry
all over your body: its red hair.
Every midnight is gorgeous as stone.
In between my legs, your kiss
touches me like tissue. Or a flower
tattered by time.

Remember the fuchsia which last summer
we hung from the eaves like lanterns
on a ship. Rocking in the wind.
Hummingbirds, small as tongues, slipped
in and around blooms being created,
being dropped—

whole and pink. At one with the air,
the grass below, and me.

*

I dance in the stillness. Like the bear
I watched rise up to tear
bark honeycombed with snow
from the branches. She staggered
on shaky back legs, filled her mouth
with cold and darkness, then lumbered
up the hillside.

*

                Each night,
I keep hold of the child I was

within, like a hood over a flower.
I rock her gently. Time
has done this, brought us close
like mother and daughter: Elizabeth
and Elizabeth.

*

All day, the sky has wept snow.
I know this is sorrow because it is silent.
It falls on me like breath. Snow is full
of solitude and so, my intoxication grows.
The fields are rich as candlelight.
I will never leave. Even though all
that's ignited dies: childhood,
my mother and father, who may be all
the way to Florida by now. The fuchsia
are dead. One or two hummingbirds
have been blown out of the sky.
Many hopes, many loves. I cross
the fields on skis. Marking
time.

At 2,000 Feet

Each day, I ski from farm to farm,
talking to no one, like an angel
necessary to none. I cast a shadow,
but so do the trees, blue against the snow
and deceptively long, as though we might
still be growing. In dreams,
I'm full of acceptance.
This could be death, certainly
someone or something has died— my soul
has overcome my spirit, the little
spirit I was born with, small
as a Baptismal dress. Whatever
nourishes the soul, kills
the self: heaven is larger
than sky. And bluer.
As I sleep, a child is lifted
from me, like torn snow.

*

My life is a quiet dance
inward. My feet, soft as fruit.
When I move, the sky,
that hard marble, moves with me.
It tosses many scarves. They fall
on men I have been blessed with:
my father, with eyes like the red dog
we loved so much. My brothers.
My brothers who hold hands
as grown men. Who are tender

as eyelids in sleep.
These men cry
as children do: their beds
large as the women they once
believed in. Because of them,
I dance slowly, soft
as snow long after
it has fallen.

*

Far inside are women. My mother's head
rolls slowly. It is stuffed with sorrow.
As such, it floats in me, some moon
uneven with grief. I hold her
within. Hemmed in
by my grandmothers' bones, white
as a dress that falls beautifully
about me. When I move
their bones move, sheer as the light
I utterly long for. Grandma Kirschner
pins green flowers to my waist,
sea-colored, like waves when turning.
Grandma Estes, at 90, pins up
my hair.

*

Nights here are tragic.
At 2,000 feet, we are touched
by all: stars falling like men
in war, the anonymous wind.
Knowledge of the world at large

comes in sleep: like letters
in the alphabet to old illiterates.
I learn the figures slowly,
half-hoping I will fail.
When I wake, it is to beauty
and dismay: millions starve
while I feast on huge
blossoms of air.

*

Like paper from which dolls
have been cut, I'm left
with holes through which
I can pass my hands.
To fill them, I take tissue
from my soul. Heavy and glutinous
from years of weeping, it's difficult
to work with. So I hang it out—
like lace on lingerie
so delicate men go crazy
whenever a strip, pink as dawn,
is revealed.

*

As my father would say, *this
is what it's all about*. But
like a clown, we thought him tragic
rather than truthful. This morning
I count raindrops on branches
thin as thread: six or eight,
such huge, shimmering burdens
seem impossible to hold. At 2,000 feet,
they are not. When they drop,

they do so in the softness of snow.
At 2,000 feet, the soul
is erotic. It dances
in the wind. Its little feet
are children on the stair.
Running up. Running down: such
music to the ear. At 2,000 feet,
nothing is wanting. Nothing
is bliss.

Robert's Arms

Within them, the world is dropped
like a marble. Small, valuable
only to the young. Dark and shining,
it rolls into something larger than itself,
as I do into Robert's arms in sleep.
Which are mortal as spring.
Like green shoots stabbing cold air.
Or snow children crush in their hands
as though each mitten-full were an angel.

       As a dancer, I learned
to hold my arms as if the world
were between them. So I hugged
time, death, self and my mother
and father in turn. As a woman,
that space is an infant: tender,
joyous and born from within.

Robert's arms hold broken rooms,
tiny as toys. In them the light goes,
like his tongue to the back of his mouth.
When I enter those rooms, street names
rush through me like trains: Sherman Road,
Woodland Lane, Sprucewood Drive,
Cottage Grove, South Street . . .

       to sit in these rooms
       is to sit in the self,
       that folding chair of soul.

I hold my own like a tiny person.
Like a starfish scooped from the sea.
My gold points rise like yellow-
tipped grasses in a field of snow.
Where horses graze slowly

until their snouts are masks of light.
Like Robert's face rising from mine.

In his arms are the hands
of time: sweeping, balletic.
They touch my own in silence.
They touch the spring, like snow
parting from the clouds.

      His arms are bent:
so are broken knees. I crawl into them—
a gardener with tools in each hand.
Some nights I wear blue, the blue
of a surgical dress and soon we're both
undone as though this house
were a hospital where any one
of us were dying.

Room upon room holds sorrow.
Bone upon bone floats in grief.
All are in this body and own,
if nothing else, its exotic parts.
A blue arm flushed with winter.
A yellow arm raised like a daffodil
in spring. Each arm is provocative:
so is loss. Both want to hold us
up . . .

      people, ghosts, angels.

      In Robert's arms,
my knees are sinking: two wet flowers
upon the snowy ground.

Broken Stars

I.

Air coasts like a blue saucer.
Like a promise: life will cost me
my life. I remember this at night,
when my bones ebb in the seaweed
of sleep. When the language of the moon
is clear and comprehensible: it spells
the light of silence, over and over,
with the letters of my name:
an "E" drawn out for eternity.

To rise from experience is to be dozens
at once. I'm 5 and putting on rubber boots
with clasps like tiny ladders. Or 13
and in a barn with boys flying from the hayloft
like dark birds upon my gentle body.
Then I'm 25 with a blue apron
spread over my hips, cooking soups.
For very little pay.

I went so far only to be driven
back. Into origins as solemn as an owl.
And sacred as a book written by a young
woman, who wrote it all
and wrote it wrong. In the end,
little is deeper, truer and more beautiful
than error. The only dart thrown
precisely, like a feather into the bird's back.
The one that bears the gift of flight.

> There have been many feathers,
> strong as my fingers. And dropped
> like clothing, with man after man.

II.

The only time I have touched God
is when I have risked being
air. When I have fallen:
into snow, into shadow, into self,
I have passed, briefly,
through God. Like snow melting
on my hands, I can endure
the cold glow life sublimely
offers. I can endure God.
Like winter light. Like mints
that make my teeth ache.

Love, though, is rooted
in history and therefore buried
in the dark. My father,
whose first gift to my mother
was an apple basket filled
with bottles of beer, as though each
were a cold branch upon which the foamy brew
would blossom. My lovers:
Carl, who in dreams slips
under my nightgown like a silver bird.
Whose feathers are blades.
Under which I never cease
to move. My lovers were error
incarnate. I gorged on them
like snow, as if each contained
an angel, or at the very least,

her white foot, her tiny
hidden smile.

I keep Carl in my dreams
the way I keep my hands:
without whom, I touch no one.

III.

Whenever I cry, a star splits in two.
Its white juice flows into the bodies
of the diminished: jellyfish
pale as hats for the dead, snakes
who hug stones as we do time,
men and women who enter one another
like trains crushing air, their children:
animals slipping out only
in darkness. Under trees
gorgeous as God. I cry
eternally and why not: it's as close
to love as I'll ever come.
That soft rain scattered in winter.
Over all the infinite snow.

Those broken stars sit in the yard
like trash: a discarded TV antenna,
the lawn chair turned over like a child
about to be spanked. After a while,
we don't even see it: only the neighbors
do.

IV.

At night, I leaf through garden books
as if each page were a painted dream.
In the season to come, I will have turtleheads,
bee balm, and monkshood. I will watch
meadowrue tremble in the wind.
I will love the anemones peaceably.
I will spend summer mornings
down on my knees, digging among all
that was buried and feared lost.
So the February cold freezes me
only as long as it lasts. Ripping
through clothes like memory.
Once I wore a pink peasant blouse.
Once I wore moccasins, soft as snow.
It was never enough. I loved a man
named Andrew. Named Scott.
Named Carl in the name
of love. With my hands,
I dug into them deeply. I dug
for loss and hit veins
of love: glorious and difficult,
its white juices stained all
I was: rain on snow, woman
on God. O intimate, green men
take off your white shirts.
Lift up your flowers. The world
as it dies needs you, your spring rivers
that flow from the broken stars.

A White Body

Like insects rare in winter.
Or the white spirit flowing about me.
The surprise of love later in life.
The body of it open. My skeleton
is a mobile, glistening. Both ghost
and being, I go on. I pass through
my mother and father and come out blue,
like a child who has swum in the ocean
too long. On the other side, I hit
space. I talk quietly.
As though the stars were wind
flowers and could be coaxed, through
patience, into bloom. But stars
are stars and I am
who I am: ready
to back down, to be female
and full of waiting.

Like a spider washed by water,
I am caught in the universe. Tumbling
over and over: webs of wind
fasten me to a thread of self.
I take my dark
limbs inward.

*

In my other body, God
is established, living alone.
I know this because I have gone off,
years at a time, into it. The one
untouched by mother and father.
The one lovers grazed, like memory.

Lift me from it and I am lifeless:
a snowflake from a field of snow.

*

Touch my ear and a dark throb
resounds. As though sex has grown there,
like a long-stemmed flower, from that other
place where roots are torn.
Touch my ear and the music
of soul begins: each side
of my heart is a white
foot, so I shuffle— soft,
older than God. Who wanted
to die young. Before the world
as a cold bulb, blossomed.
Before the heavy petals
fell, like dust.

But I, like God, wasn't able
to die just yet. So a son
came out in a white body.
So a son was placed on my bones.
Given up, like milk
from a cow. This is luxury:
to let another die for you.
And then go on, as though such deaths
were historical, intended.

In character. Which we never
fall out of. In dreams,
my teeth are knocked out—
my mouth hums with emptiness
and blood. In love,
it is my breath that goes,

completely, into the other.
My lungs work like hands:
red, chapped from the cold
that is so continuous
in these parts. And the hands,
as we know them, are bird-like
with belief: they are forever
on the rise.

*

I want a son in a white
body. Spread like a picnic cloth
over time. Already he wears
my mother's blue shoes. He walks
through snow, through soul
into the world of me. I meet him
in the face of his father. In trees
which baa-in-wind like lambs.
In the thread of frost scratched
on the windowpane. The one that
stitches me to myself, like two sides
of the same dress. He makes pain
feel like wonder. And God
look like Jesus— deceptively beautiful
and descended into life. To be like
one of us— going in
as we go out.

*

I lie on my stomach on the bed
and let a man touch me,
draw in and out what he wants,
what he is afraid to have.

The sky watches. Silence
watches. My hands, cupped
between my legs, catch
whatever passes.

*

I'm without my mother and father,
my brothers, my sister; their children.
Their backs are stairs of snow:
I climb slowly to blue
vistas, deep as paintings.
They are with the first snow melt—
gone quickly and all at once.
I am with absence. Soon
the summer air will be charged
with it: with relief it will cut
the gross greenery that mats trees
like flesh. The gross greenery
that is God. Can you kill
leaves? Can you slit their stems
like throats? I would do this
for you: Mother, Father,
Sister, Brother, Husband,
Newborn. If it would bring
you into me, through me,
out of me. I have split
myself open to touch
God: you are what it cost.

Yellow Streamers

They are tied to trees, marked
for death. So is my grandmother
in sleep. Cut to the quick
in spring. In me, they fall:
feathers onto a bird's back.
Snapped thread. My mother
calls: what's wrong? Has Robert
left you? *Mom, Mom,*
our woods are full of sweet
young things with yellow streamers
tied to their waists. We are killing
them quickly. We kill them
to let in the light. For firewood
for next year's winter. It's
terrible, terrible. These falling
trees. The inevitable death
of my grandmother. Yellow streamers
unwrapped from our hands
like whips, or things
of beauty.

Tap Lines

Here runs sweetness as though
from ourselves. As though we, too,
were willing to bleed the clear light.
In Los Angeles, young gang women
kill for drugs. I might do the same
for this: the sugars of grief, soft
as my fingertips. Drops of it
roll down my body like come.
Slow as spring. As mercy
when we ask for it. In hospitals,
body after body gives up its life.
A child is born dead. So
are stones. And yet
we pick them up with our hands.
Tap lines run between trees
like Chinese jump ropes: purple
and teal. I don't even know
how it goes. An old person—
your grandfather— is opening
his wrists. I don't even know
how it goes. Just that it runs:
the sap, the spring.

Lesser Animals

When the door of this page closes,
experience opens: fundamental
in its question—*can we
go on?* Think
before you answer.
It's not so easy.
Beauty turns us
from inner
pain. From the lesser
animals who love us.
Down at the bottom, the dark
mite grows. All mouth,
no soul. Like lovers
I have known. Who have raped
me for leaving them.
The earth knows this story.
History does. Yesterday
we burned wood and brush
from trees just felled.
I tell you the wood
was singing. Like martyrs
joyous in their deaths.
O happy wood, teach me
your song. Your high whistle.
Your deadly joy.

Carnegie Mellon Poetry

1975
The Living and the Dead, Ann Hayes
In the Face of Descent, T. Alan Broughton

1976
The Week the Dirigible Came, Jay Meek
Full of Lust and Good Usage, Stephen Dunn

1977
How I Escaped from the Labyrinth and Other Poems,
    Philip Dacey
The Lady from the Dark Green Hills, Jim Hall
For Luck: Poems 1962-1977, H.L. Van Brunt
By the Wreckmaster's Cottage, Paula Rankin

1978
New & Selected Poems, James Bertolino
The Sun Fetcher, Michael Dennis Browne
A Circus of Needs, Stephen Dunn
The Crowd Inside, Elizabeth Libbey

1979
Paying Back the Sea, Philip Dow
Swimmer in the Rain, Robert Wallace
Far from Home, T. Alan Broughton
The Room Where Summer Ends, Peter Cooley
No Ordinary World, Mekeel McBride

1980
And the Man Who Was Traveling Never Got Home,
    H.L. Van Brunt
Drawing on the Walls, Jay Meek
The Yellow House on the Corner, Rita Dove
The 8-Step Grapevine, Dara Wier
The Mating Reflex, Jim Hall

1981
A Little Faith, John Skoyles
Augers, Paula Rankin
Walking Home from the Icehouse, Vern Rutsala
Work and Love, Stephen Dunn
The Rote Walker, Mark Jarman
Morocco Journal, Richard Harteis
Songs of a Returning Soul, Elizabeth Libbey

1982
The Granary, Kim R. Stafford
Calling the Dead, C.G. Hanzlicek
Dreams Before Sleep, T. Alan Broughton
Sorting It Out, Anne S. Perlman
Love Is Not a Consolation; It Is a Light, Primus St. John

1983
The Going Under of the Evening Land, Mekeel McBride
Museum, Rita Dove
Air and Salt, Eve Shelnutt
Nightseasons, Peter Cooley

1984
Falling from Stardom, Jonathan Holden
Miracle Mile, Ed Ochester
Girlfriends and Wives, Robert Wallace
Earthly Purposes, Jay Meek
Not Dancing, Stephen Dunn
The Man in the Middle, Gregory Djanikian
A Heart Out of This World, David James
All You Have in Common, Dara Wier

1985
Smoke from the Fires, Michael Dennis Browne
Full of Lust and Good Usage, Stephen Dunn (2nd edition)
Far and Away, Mark Jarman

Anniversary of the Air, Michael Waters
To the House Ghost, Paula Rankin
Midwinter Transport, Anne Bromley

1986
Seals in the Inner Harbor, Brendan Galvin
Thomas and Beulah, Rita Dove
Further Adventures With You, C.D. Wright
Fifteen to Infinity, Ruth Fainlight
False Statements, Jim Hall
When There Are No Secrets, C.G. Hanzlicek

1987
Some Gangster Pain, Gillian Conoley
Other Children, Lawrence Raab
Internal Geography, Richard Harteis
The Van Gogh Notebook, Peter Cooley
A Circus of Needs, Stephen Dunn (2nd edition)
Ruined Cities, Vern Rutsala
Places and Stories, Kim R. Stafford

1988
Preparing to Be Happy, T. Alan Broughton
Red Letter Days, Mekeel McBride
The Abandoned Country, Thomas Rabbitt
The Book of Knowledge, Dara Wier
Changing the Name to Ochester, Ed Ochester
Weaving the Sheets, Judith Root

1989
Recital in a Private Home, Eve Shelnutt
A Walled Garden, Michael Cuddihy
The Age of Krypton, Carol J. Pierman
Land That Wasn't Ours, David Keller
Stations, Jay Meek
The Common Summer: New and Selected Poems,
    Robert Wallace

The Burden Lifters, Michael Waters
Falling Deeply into America, Gregory Djanikian
Entry in an Unknown Hand, Franz Wright

1990
Why the River Disappears, Marcia Southwick
Staying Up For Love, Leslie Adrienne Miller
Dreamer, Primus St. John

1991
Permanent Change, John Skoyles
Clackamas, Gary Gildner
Tall Stranger, Gillian Conoley
The Gathering of My Name, Cornelius Eady
A Dog in a Lifeboat, Joyce Pesseroff
Raised Underground, Renate Wood
Divorce: A Romance, Paula Rankin

1992
Modern Ocean, James Harms
The Astonished Hours, Peter Cooley
You Won't Remember This, Michael Dennis Browne
Twenty Colors, Elizabeth Kirschner
First A Long Hesitation, Eve Shelnutt
Bountiful, Michael Waters
All That Heat in a Cold Sky, Elizabeth Libbey